Sophie's Story

A Guide to Selective Mutism

By Vera Joffe, Ph.D.

Illustrated by Margaret Scott

Edited by Monica Iachan

First Edition

Sophie's Story: A Guide to Selective Mutism.

Library of Congress Control Number: 2007901104
ISBN-13:978-0-9787542-1-1
ISBN-10:0-9787542-1-2
Requests for books should contact:
www.verajoffe.com
(954) 341-4441

This "Purple Book" is dedicated to my "Lavender Heart Connection": My Daughters Melissa and Monica.

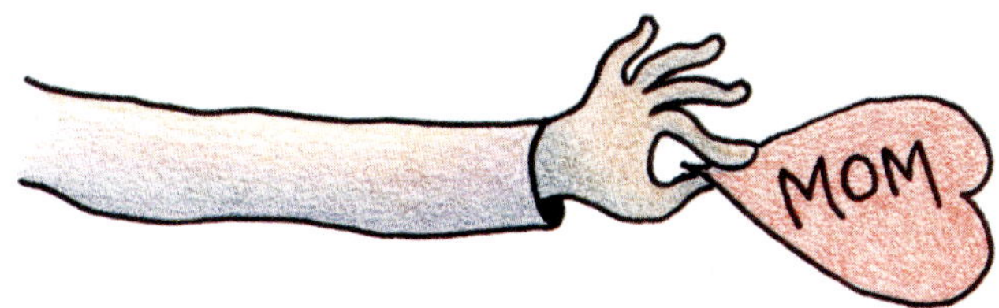

Thank You Notes: *I would like to thank Margaret Scott for being a wonderful partner in this project: Her sensibility and understanding of the topic was reflected in her wonderful pictures in this book. And I want to thank Monica for always reviewing my work, and for making my message more clear, and for correcting my English (still not my first language).*
I am also grateful to Lucy Morales who made the final review and editing of this manuscript. Also, to all the children, parents and teachers who worked as a "team" for the best understanding, treatment, and quality of life of children with Selective Mutism.

I was honored when Dr. Peter Jensen accepted to review and to write the Foreword of this book. Finally, I would like to acknowledge the guidance of Dr. Elisa Shipon-Blum whose passion, knowledge and dedication to the area of Selective Mutism inspired me more to work in this area, and to write this book.

Sophie's Story: A Guide to Selective Mutism

Chapter 1: One Week Before School

To my new teacher,

I am really happy to be starting school this year! I can't wait to learn all kinds of things and to meet the kids in my class!

This is a picture of me. This is what I look like:

My parents told me I am more than ready to start school. These are some things that I like to play with:

Dolls

LEGOs

Crayons and markers

Dress-up clothes

Chapter 2: When I Was a Little Girl

My parents told me nice things about me when I was a very little girl. They said I had a wonderful smile. They also told me that I loved to follow my mother around the kitchen when she would bake cookies. Sometimes, when there was a very loud noise (like when a fire truck passed by), I would start crying. They thought it was because my ears hurt.

My parents told me that once I started talking, I would not stop. I would talk, talk, and talk nonstop. They were so happy! They said I was going to be a television star — somebody who reports the news or the weather on television, something like that. Or that I would have a talk show. But sometimes when people would come close to me, and look into my beautiful eyes and say, "Oh, you are such a cute little girl!" I was a little shy, and I would look away, or even cry.

I have always wanted to be an artist, an actress, or a singer. This is how I think I would look if I became a famous singer, just like one of the singers in the popular talent show on television:

Chapter 3: Preschool

When I was four years old, I went to my first school. It was called "A Nice World." I loved my teacher, Ms. Fern. When I got to school she would always be waiting for me with a big smile. And I loved the people in the front office, like Mrs. Pam and Ms. JoAnne.

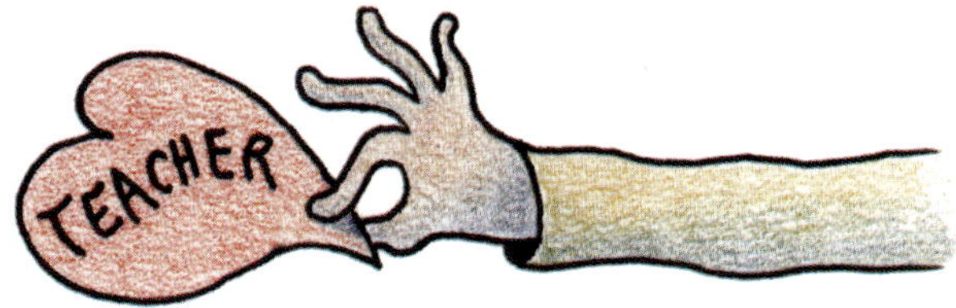

We had music every week and also gym. I loved my preschool so much. I sang, played with my friends, and looked forward to arts and crafts. I loved when Ms. Fern would read to us. When we celebrated Thanksgiving we had so much fun! And on Mother's Day, we would make cards and sing to our mommies. We liked that school so much that I stayed there another year, for Kindergarten. And I was so lucky! Ms Fern was my teacher again, and I knew all the kids in my class.

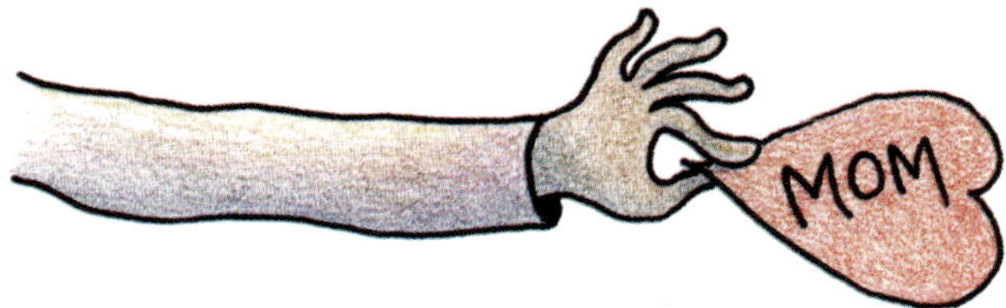

I loved singing, but I could only hear my voice singing so loudly when I was at home singing in front of the mirror. When I was at school I didn't like to be in the front row! Here is a picture of me singing at home, in front of the mirror, practicing for the Thanksgiving celebration and show at school.

Chapter 4: A Year Passed Quickly. But Then, What Happened?

The year went by so fast! Suddenly, it was summer. We had our end-of-the-year celebration, and then… we said our goodbyes, and summer started.

My parents took me on a long vacation to see our relatives in New York. I got to see the big dinosaur at the museum, and I also went to a very tall building in New York. The elevator went up, and up, and up… I thought we would never get to the top of the building to see the city! I felt a little sick going up the elevator, but my dad was playing some rhyming games with me, so I forgot about my fear for a while.

When we came back from vacation, my mom and dad told me that I was going to "summer camp." I didn't know what "summer camp" was all about. My parents told me that it was a place close to our house, and that I was going to have fun there. I was going to

meet new kids, we were going to swim every day, and I was going to do arts and crafts. Then, after lunch, in the middle of the day, Mommy was going to pick me up from camp, and we were going to have more fun.

It was good to know what I was going to do at camp, but there was so much about it that I didn't know… I felt a little nervous. I kept thinking about my school, my friends, my day at school. What was summer camp, anyway?

The day came when it was time to go to camp. Mommy and Daddy took me to that other place, a big place. They showed me the pool. I felt so small standing by the diving board. A lot of kids were coming to the camp at the same time, and there was a lot of noise.

This nice lady came to meet me, and she said she was going to be my counselor. Her name was Sandra. She was pretty nice. Then my mom said, "This is Sophie, and this is her first time at summer camp, right Sophie?" And my mom looked at me, waiting for an answer.

Something happened: I froze, and I just nodded and looked away. My mom did not see, but I got a very nervous feeling at that moment. She did not notice that I could not get the words out. I just couldn't do it. My body froze and I felt like I could not say a word, although I wanted to say "hello" so much!

Then Sandra told my parents that it was time for them to leave and that camp was about to start. Sandra told her group of kids (about 10) that we were going to a room in a big, beautiful blue building. She also had a helper, Karina, with her. And so we all went to the building. I was still feeling so nervous! I felt like I couldn't even walk, or move. But I followed Ms. Sandra.

Chapter 5: Summer Camp: Alone, and in Silence.

From that moment on, I just could not talk anymore. Not to Sandra, not to Karina, not to any kid. I was very nervous at camp. I even knew a girl in my group. She lived on my block and we saw each other every day on the street playing with our moms. She smiled a lot and sat with me. I really wanted to ask her to play, but I was scared.

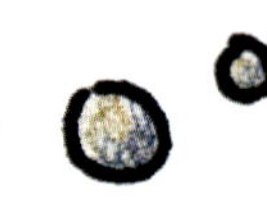

I think Sandra knew that I was afraid to be around the other kids, since she would hold my hand a lot. I wanted to tell her to call my mom, but I could not say anything. I knew my friends were confused, and I wished I could tell them that I felt scared, but words just would not come out. I wanted to go home. I didn't like the big camp.

I didn't even let my counselor know when I needed to go to the bathroom. I just went whenever someone else went, and the counselor let me go as the other kid's "buddy", but it was my "silent" way to just go without having to ask by talking.

The minute I got in my mom's car after camp, I told her everything I did at camp — about the kids, the counselors. But I looked a little sad, my mom said.

My mom and dad did not know that I was quiet and shy at camp, and I was afraid to tell them.

I was afraid they would be mad at me, and that they would tell me I needed to talk or that they would be upset, and that they would not understand. But I wanted to make friends with the other kids, I wanted them to like me, but just being with new girls was kind of scary, and words would not come out!

Chapter 6: Silence Talks: What's the Matter?

Then one day, I was playing with a girl in my group, and she asked me a question: "What do you want to draw?" I tried to answer with gestures, and by making faces, but she got angry because I would not talk to her, and she hit me. I started crying (but without making any noise; there were just tears in my eyes). That was when the counselor called my parents to talk to them about what was happening at camp. I was not talking. I just *chose* not to talk at camp and they didn't know what to do to help me. They also said they thought I looked sad during "circle time" and during free play. They noticed that I did not play with any kids who were playing a "word game" but that I liked to run with the kids around the playground as long as I did not have to say a word in order to play with them.

This is a picture of me playing alone during "free time."

My parents were very sad and upset, and they did not know what to do. They talked to me and I told them that I was nervous at camp. I was afraid the kids would laugh at me or make too much noise! I was so shy. I did not know how to explain this to my parents, but they understood. They really did. Daddy told me that he had been afraid to be around a lot of people for as long as he could remember. He was also scared to talk in front of people when he was a little kid, and even when he was a teenager. But today my dad is the head of a company and he said he has to talk in front of a lot of people. My father said he is still nervous, but he does it. I wish I could do it too. It would be so much easier.

Camp came and went. Then we went back to New York to my older cousin's wedding. I was the ring girl for the wedding. I was so excited. I had a special dress, and I knew that I was going to have my hair done for the wedding, just like big girls do. I was feeling so good! I could not wait.

We went to New York a couple of days early because there was what they called a "Rehearsal Dinner." We went to the hall and the grownups told me that I needed to walk here and there, and that I needed to carry a pillow with rings on it. I got really nervous. I was so afraid of making mistakes! I was afraid I was going to fall and drop the rings. The hall was so big and there were so many people in there that I felt like I was going to freeze again.

After I walked with the pillow with the rings, a lot of grownups came to me and told me, "Oh, you are so cute! You look adorable!" I froze! I wanted my mom and dad, but where were they? I could not see them! And then my aunt came and kissed me, and this other woman (I didn't even know who she was) came and hugged me. I was nervous, very nervous.

That's also when I stopped talking to strangers. I just talked to my mom, my dad, my cousin, and my aunt. Nobody else. I felt really bad, and my mom and dad were worried about me. But they helped me. When someone asked me a question, they would answer for me, and then they would say, "She is a little shy. Please, don't take it personally!" I know they were trying to help me, but I felt even worse after that. But at least I did not have to answer questions.

Chapter 7: Finding People Who Can Help

After we came back from the wedding in New York, my mom and dad called my doctor, Dr. Angel. He told my parents that we should go to see a "talking doctor," Doctor Malka, who might be able to help me a little.

When I heard Dr. Malka was a "talking doctor," I was really afraid. I thought she was going to give me a shot to make me talk, or if I didn't talk, she was going to put some medicine down my throat to make me talk. But boy, was I wrong!

Doctor Malka saw my parents, and then I went the next day. She talked to me and she did not look at me. She started drawing and I joined her. I spent some more time with Doctor Malka who would draw and play games with me and with my parents. Slowly, Doctor Malka and I started playing games by ourselves, and then I felt more comfortable with her. We started playing UNO and Guess Who? and I did not even realize that the longer I was there, the more at ease I felt with Dr. Malka.

I could not believe my ears. I talked to Dr. Malka about the wedding in New York, and about feeling nervous around new people and how hard it was to talk to strangers. I also told her how sad I felt at camp when I ended up playing by myself on the playground.

I felt Dr. Malka understood that I really wanted to be like other kids at camp and at school. I wanted not to feel nervous, but I couldn't. We talk about all my fears. I told her that I am afraid that kids will make fun of me, or that they will make a lot of noise if I talk. I am also afraid of talking funny. I don't know, I'm just afraid.

Chapter 8: Selective Mutism

Dr. Malka told my parents that I have this thing called "Selective Mutism." She said that sometimes children like me, with SM (Selective Mutism) are afraid (anxious) of being around some people and of talking to them in some places while they talk to others, like their parents at home. Being in school and talking to other kids and with the teacher is a scary situation for little kids like me. She also said that what I have is also called "Social-Communication Anxiety Disorder" by some doctors who work with kids like me.

Dr. Malka said that there are many things all of us can do to help me with my fear of being and talking in the classroom. I say "all of us" because I am so lucky to have Mommy and Daddy, you, Dr. Malka, and everyone who will help me in the classroom. Dr. Malka said we will try to take "baby steps," and that little by little I will feel more comfortable there.

One of the things she suggested was for me to come to school and meet you before the school year starts so that I won't be so nervous on the first day of school. I will know where things are in the room, and I will feel more at home. I am so happy that you are reading this book because I would like to come to school one day the week before classes start. Maybe I can help you get ready in the classroom by making some pictures or decorations for the walls! I love drawing, and my mommy told me that I am very good at it. Coming to your class and meeting you before school will help me because:

a. I will get to meet you and find out more about you.
b. I will get used to the classroom, and I will know where everything is.
c. I will be more familiar with the school, and I will find out where the bathroom is, where the cafeteria is, and where the nurse's office is.

If you can, I would love for you to come to my house so that I can show you all the toys I have and for you to meet my doggie, Marshmallow. Maybe if you come to my house, I will feel more comfortable talking or playing with you in my own place, where I don't feel nervous.

Chapter 9: Other Things I Worry About School That Maybe You Can Help Me With:

I hope by now you understand that if I don't talk it's not because I am being "a bad girl" and I am trying to get away with things. I just have what Dr. Malka calls "anxiety" about some places and people, and about talking. And I won't be able to start feeling comfortable talking all at once, so we have to take baby steps.

I may have to sign to you in the beginning to ask for certain things, like going to the bathroom.

I am so afraid I won't be able to ask to go to the bathroom! During summer camp, I had a couple of accidents when we were playing outside. I wanted to go to the bathroom, but I couldn't tell the counselor (because I was afraid to talk), so I just wet my pants and the other kids made fun of me… I was so embarrassed! Do you think that we can have a little "code" or "sign" for me to ask you to go to the bathroom? I would really be happy if you let me do that.

If anyone in the class starts making fun of me or gets upset that I don't talk, can you please explain that it's not because I am mean, have bad manners, or that I am playing games? I will feel so much better when I know that you will be helping me with the kids in the classroom. I want to make friends and to talk and play just like any other little kid in your new class. I just wish I could feel free to play and make new friends easily.

There is another little thing I would like to ask you: When we are in circle time, it's hard if I am sitting right in front of you and you talk to me looking at me in the eye. Can I sit next to you? I feel less afraid when you are talking to me and not looking in my eyes. Thank you for understanding this.

Also, can you not put me on the spot during circle time?
Can I let you know when (and if) I will be able to talk in circle time? Maybe I will raise my hand when nobody is looking at me. And if I am too scared to speak, will you let me use gestures to tell you what I need to tell you (like when I need to go to the bathroom)? Maybe with time I will be a kid just like any other kid in my grade: I want so much to be like the other kids!

I don't know if my mommy and daddy told you, but I am very sensitive to loud noises. As a matter of fact, one of the worst day of the year for me is the 4th of July. I love watching the fireworks, but I get so upset when I hear the noise!

So we all stay home, and we watch the fireworks on TV and I put the volume really low so that I don't get upset. Next year I will use my earplugs and I will try to go outside with my family to see the fireworks.

In preschool, I started getting really scared of fire drills, so the director of the school, Ms. Randy, decided to ask me to be her "fire drill helper."

She would come to my classroom and ask me to follow her to the office. Then she would tell me that we were going to have a fire drill and that it was going to be loud and she would have me push the button for the drill. I loved doing that, because I got to help Ms. Randy and I also knew when the loud noise was going to start so I was not that afraid. The noise still bothered me, but at least I wasn't surprised.

Sometimes I don't like to eat certain foods.

So if I don't eat the lunch at school, can you just send a note to my parents, but not put me on the spot in the cafeteria? Thank you very much.

Chapter 10: The End, but the Beginning of a Very Nice Year!

I want to thank you very much for reading my little book on my fears about being around and talking to some people and in some places. When school starts, I will try my best to feel comfortable but I am not sure when I will be comfortable enough to bring words out right away with you, or with the kids in the classroom. I hope that you will let me come to school and visit you before the first day of school.

Dr. Malka gave my mom and dad the names of other books about "Selective Mutism," and she also said that you could go to the computer and find out about those books (written by Dr. Elisa Shipon-Blum) and a lot more about Selective Mutism. You just have to go to

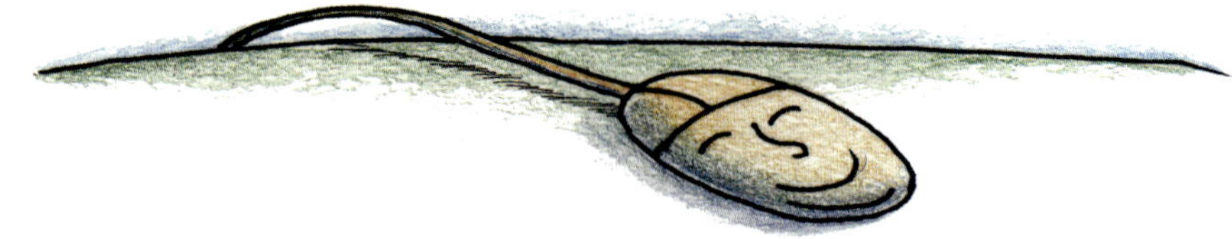

www.selectivemutism.org. Please see the names of other books at the end of my book.

I feel good knowing that you understand me better now.

I am so happy that I am starting a new year at school, and even though I am really scared, I know that I have my "team helpers," like you, my mom and dad, and Dr. Malka. If we can all work together to help me in the beginning, I may feel less afraid to be starting a new school year, meeting new friends, and having a new teacher: you!

From your student,

Sophie.

A Final Word to Parents and Teachers

I hope that with this little book you can learn more about Selective Mutism. Over the last five years, more scientific research has been conducted to study this very complex condition, Selective Mutism, and how it is very closely connected with Social and Communication Anxiety Disorder. We hope that we will learn more about Selective Mutism as more rigorous scientific studies are completed. In the meantime, you as parents and teachers can help children with Selective Mutism by educating other people about this condition.

This book is about Sophie, and your child may share some characteristics with her. However, if you want, you may use this book as a guide to write a similar book about your child to present to her or his teacher.

Your knowledge about Selective Mutism, support of your child, and willingness to share information with the educational staff that will work with your child in the upcoming academic year are very important. It is essential that you help all the people who will work with your child to understand that Selective Mutism has strong links to Social-Communication Anxiety: Children with Selective Mutism have difficulties not only with "not speaking at school," but they are also anxious about communicating in other situations. They may also have higher sensitivity (such as to noise, touch, foods) than other children. The initial goal in helping these children is not to make them talk, but to help them feel more comfortable and less anxious in school and in other places.

It would be very helpful if you introduce information about Selective Mutism and Social Anxiety to all the teachers and other people in contact with your child, such as a ballet teacher, sports coach, and the religion teacher. Make sure you inform other persons involved in your child's daily life (including extended family members and neighbors). Please do not forget the cafeteria staff at school (your child may want to order food or ice cream but not be able to do so for fear of going to the ice cream table and initiating conversation).

As in the story of Sophie, it is important to develop a team of people to work with you and with your child: your family, the teacher (and school personnel), and maybe a professional in the area. Once you have your team, the professional can help you develop a plan to help your child become more comfortable with people in various situations. Here is an example of a plan for a fictitious child with Selective Mutism:

1. Daniel was in 3rd grade in a public school. His native language was not English. He spoke only with his parents, and only at home. He spoke in his native language in other places, but he did not say a word at school. Daniel ate only cream-colored foods and he was very sensitive

to loud noises. He was very afraid that the school was going to have a fire drill because he did not like the noise the alarm made.

2. The family consulted with a child psychologist who visited the school, and talked to the guidance counselor and the teacher. The psychologist provided educational information about Selective Mutism to the school personnel, and she worked with them on the day of the visit and observation. The family, teacher, and psychologist made notes on the child's communication chart at the beginning of the multidisciplinary intervention.

3. The team took notes on the following: the *type of communication* (nonverbal, whispering, speaking with a regular volume of voice), *with whom the child communicated* (including nonverbal tools) *, the place, and the activity that the child was engaged in* when the communication took place.

4. The psychologist helped the team understand that Daniel's difficulties were not limited to "not speaking" at school. For instance, the team decided to let Daniel know when there was going to be a fire drill at school. In fact, they told Daniel that he would be the "principal's helper" in setting the alarm off for the whole school. In this way, the team reassured Daniel that he would know in advance when the "alarm noise" was coming, and Daniel felt very important because he was able to help with the fire drill. He could also wear earplugs when he set off the alarm. Slowly, Daniel became more tolerant to the noise of the drill.

5. The team discussed the notes on Daniel's communication chart and decided which activity, location, and person would be appropriate for the intervention to take place for this little boy. For instance, Daniel was very comfortable playing with and talking to his older sister, Julia. Julia was invited to go to the psychologist's office to play games with Daniel. This activity facilitated the work in the psychologist's office and it made it easier for Daniel to start communicating more comfortably with children in his classroom.

6. Daniel's favorite classmates were invited to his house. After a few play dates, Daniel started speaking with his mother in front of some of the children. He then started talking softly to one of the friends who came to his house to play in the swimming pool.

7. It is important to work slowly, to have patience, and to not draw attention to your child when she or he speaks for the first time in a new situation and with a new person. This usually puts a lot of pressure on a child who suffers from anxiety. Daniel's parents were careful to provide him with a comfortable setting in which to develop his relationships without feeling overwhelmed.

8. After a few weeks the team met again to see if the communication chart had changed and if Daniel had expanded the locations, situations of interaction, and people with whom he communicated. The team also discussed whether Daniel was feeling less anxious, and if his nonverbal behaviors were indicating that he was feeling more comfortable at school and in other situations that he was afraid of before. Daniel was trying new foods in the cafeteria at school. His parents decided to let him purchase lunch twice a week at school if he was willing to try the foods that were being offered.

9. Daniel's parents discussed the results further with the psychologist and they consulted with his pediatrician and other doctors to decide whether they should consider other treatment approaches to working with his social anxiety and fears (including medication).

10. With time, Daniel became more comfortable in additional situations, and he spoke to more people. For instance, a few weeks after intervention and treatment started, Daniel went to a fast-food restaurant with his father and he ordered French fries all by himself. He also spoke with a neighbor who was selling Girl Scout cookies.

Sophie's and Daniel's stories are just a couple of examples of the importance of the building a team to help a child with Selective Mutism (and Social-Communication Anxiety Disorder). When using the step-by-step approach, remember that the goal of intervention is not to make the child speak, but to help her or him feel more comfortable in social situations.

Here are some resources for you to read, and for the team of people working with your child:

The websites www.selectivemutism.org and www.childhoodanxietynetwork.org are wonderful sources of information and reference materials. The websites above also have information about Dr. Elisa Shipon-Blum's books on Selective Mutism and information about Education Interventions, and Rights.

McHolm, A.E.; Cunningham, C.E.; Vanier, M.K. (2005). *Helping your child with Selective Mutism*. Oakland: New Harbinger Publications.

Cline, T. & Baldwin, S. (2004). *Selective Mutism in Children.* (second edition). London: Whurr Publishers.

Good luck, and please, write or e-mail if you have any questions or suggestions,

Sincerely,

Vera Joffe, Ph.D.
(www.verajoffe.com)